| P I | | G U I D E |

HEREFORD

PILGRIM · GUIDE

HEREFORD

Michael Tavinor

Illustrated by
Dominic Harbour

CANTERBURY
PRESS
Norwich

For John and Meriel Oliver

Text © Michael Tavinor 2003
Illustrations © Dominic Harbour 2003

First published in 2003 by the Canterbury Press Norwich
(a publishing imprint of Hymns Ancient & Modern Limited,
a registered charity)
St Mary's Works, St Mary's Plain,
Norwich, Norfolk NR3 3BH

www.scm-canterburypress.co.uk

British Library Cataloguing in Publication Data

A catalogue record for this book is available
from the British Library

Every effort has been made to trace copyright
ownership of items in this book. The publisher would be
grateful to be informed of any omissions

ISBN 1-85311-546-0

Typeset by Rowland Phototypesetting Ltd,
Bury St Edmunds, Suffolk
Printed and bound in Great Britain by
Bookmarque Ltd, Croydon

Contents

A plan of Hereford Cathedral

KEY TO PLAN

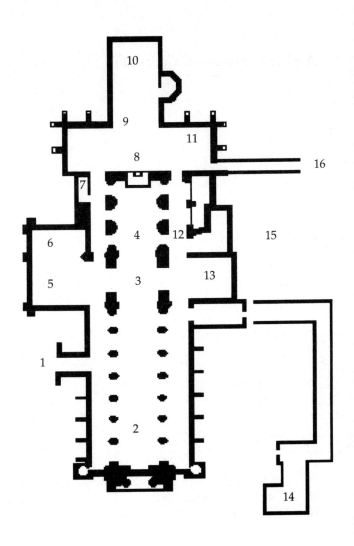

vii

Introduction

The first *Pilgrim Guide* I wrote was on Tewkesbury Abbey and that came out of a long association with that great church. I write this new guide to Hereford Cathedral conscious that I do so having been Dean here for not yet one year. Many others are more qualified than I to write on the history and the spirituality of this ancient and beautiful place of prayer.

Yet places of pilgrimage are also places of immediacy. While it is humbling to be part of a community for many years and to be discovering new things about it years later, it is certain that so many who come to our great cathedrals and churches today simply don't have opportunity for this leisured exploration. Many who come as visitors are with us for a matter of hours, even minutes, and those of us who have the care of such churches are in the business of helping others to glimpse something of the pilgrimage in their visit – however short that may be.

My hope is that this little book may be of use to those who, like me, are new to Hereford and that it may also suggest – to those who know and love it well – new ways of using the Cathedral as a source of prayer and inspiration.

The Porch

We are about to begin a journey – a journey of discovery – and, as in so many spiritual experiences, we need to be prepared, to have our minds attuned to see the deeper meaning of this Cathedral and its story. The Porch is thus a threshold – from the outside world, with all its business and concerns, into the Cathedral, with its own message and challenge.

Pilgrims have been crossing this threshold since before the Norman Conquest, although the Porch we enter today is of more recent date.

Hereford's Porch is one of the largest in England. In fact there are two porches, one leading into the other. The inner Porch was built in the 1280s and had an upper chamber with an altar dedicated to the Blessed Virgin Mary. Added to this is the beautiful Booth Porch, completed in 1518, its many windows allowing light to flood the upper chamber in which there would have been another Chapel, this one with an altar dedicated to St Saviour. A document dating from the period when the porch was being built declares certain indulgences, or 'spiritual gifts', to be granted to all who said prayers in this Chapel.

Much the same will happen on the journey we begin today. We modern-day pilgrims bring our own

1

gifts – our lives – which we offer as best we can. And we receive back the blessings which this Cathedral has to offer – peace, stillness, beauty, colour, welcome, challenge.

> *God of welcome,*
> *Receive what we bring*
> *Accept what we are*
> *Challenge what we have been*
> *Inspire what we can become*
> *Through Jesus Christ our Lord.*

The Nave

At first sight, when we enter the Cathedral, we seem to be entering a forest. Large trees march relentlessly, light from the windows changes patterns on the forest floor, and above, the vault seems like a canopy of branches and leaves, interweaving and combining. When we look at the tops of the pillars, we see naturalistic carvings – motifs derived from forest foliage – here interpreted in warm sandstone, itself the colour of the surrounding countryside, with its ploughed fields and ever-changing textures.

Perhaps we shouldn't wonder that medieval craftsmen used the natural world as inspiration for their work. For them, the medieval universe was understood as a cosmos in which all things were linked. Human beings, animals and plants, stars, angels and saints were parts of the one great design of God. Entering a great church like this is to enter mystery, but it is not a mystery cut off from the world outside. Both church and world are linked under God.

As we enter this forest, with all its majesty and its grandeur, we pause to give thanks for the majesty and beauty of God, seen in the natural world and in monuments created by humankind's skill and ingenuity. We pause to remember ways in which we have failed

The Nave

to cherish the natural order; as we marvel at the 'forest' of this Cathedral's Nave, we know that millions of acres of primeval forest are daily being cut down in so many parts of the world – hardwoods providing a huge profit but whose loss is damaging the world's ecology.

> *Lord, help us to use what you give us*
> *With gratitude, reverence and care.*
> *Help us to pass on to others a world of beauty and*
>   *generosity.*
> *Self-giving God, help us to give first of ourselves*
> *So that others may live.*

The Nave looks solid and permanent, but it was not always so. Even apparently strong and secure structures may suffer collapse. Despite efforts to secure the West Tower throughout the eighteenth century, on Easter Monday in 1786 it fell, bringing with it half the Nave which was left open to the sky.

Two years later, James Wyatt, an architect of national repute, was called in. He offered designs to repair the Cathedral, and what we see today is largely the result of his restoration – and those of L. N. Cottingham and Sir George Gilbert Scott, the architects who followed him.

Aesthetic and structural reasons, together with lack of funds, caused the Chapter to ask for the Nave to be rebuilt one bay shorter than it had been, and Wyatt destroyed what remained of the two upper storeys, substituting a design of his own with timber and plaster vaulting.

When disaster strikes great buildings, there is always discussion as to the style the rebuilding should take. At the time of writing, many designs are being submitted for a memorial or building on the site of the twin towers of the World Trade Center in New York. Sometimes, the disaster allows opportunity for new vision – the great example of this is the building of Alan of Walsingham's Octagon at Ely, after the disastrous collapse of the central tower in 1322.

It is interesting to compare ways in which German and British towns were rebuilt after the destruction of the Second World War. Often, in Germany, buildings were replaced to resemble as closely as possible the destroyed structure, while in Britain, new and ultra-modern work was often thrown up, extolling the 'brave new world'.

In the event, Wyatt followed the existing design in his rebuilding of the Nave, but used a plain, elegant Gothic style for the new west front. It was admired by some but criticized by others for being too lightweight and precisely because it was not in keeping with the Romanesque style of what had preceded it.

> Lord God, ever old and ever new,
> Alpha and Omega – our beginning and our end.
> Give us respect for what has been
> Courage to embrace what shall be
> And wisdom to see you in all things.

Maps of the Diocese of Hereford

The Cathedral is so called because it contains the 'cathedra' or seat of the Bishop, and is thus the 'mother church' of the diocese. Hereford Diocese was founded in the seventh century and is one of the oldest in England. The Diocese covers the whole of Herefordshire, South Shropshire and a few parishes in Wales which were given the choice in 1920, when the Welsh Church was disestablished, of becoming part of the new Church in Wales or part of the Diocese of Hereford.

The maps of the Diocese in the north aisle show the huge area covered – from as far south as Ross-on-Wye to ten miles north-west of Shrewsbury, and from the Welsh borders to the Malvern Hills. Hereford is probably the most rural of all English dioceses and we are proud of our agricultural tradition, our rolling hills and the magnificent rivers which water the countryside.

This County doth share as deep as any in the alphabet of our English Commodities through excelling in W for Wood, Wheat, Wool and Water. And seeing God hath blessed this County with so many Ws, we wish the inhabitants thereof the continuance and increase of one more – Wisdom.

Thomas Fuller (1608–1661)

The Corona

Our eye is now caught by the Corona above the altar at the tower crossing. It provides a striking division between the Nave – the 'people's church' – and the Chancel or Quire, and is one of the most important recent additions to the Cathedral. From 1863 until 1967, this division was marked by a screen, designed by Sir George Gilbert Scott and made by the Coventry metalworking firm of Francis Skidmore. Many medieval cathedrals and churches had or have screens which divide the church into several 'rooms' and help to create a sense of mystery, and Hereford had such a medieval screen until the eighteenth century. Hereford's Victorian screen, being of open metalwork, didn't divide the Cathedral completely and it was still possible to use the Nave and Chancel together. But the ravages of time had their effect on the screen and by the 1960s it had become tarnished and damaged. In addition, liturgical change moved towards greater openness and approachability.

The screen was removed and put into storage. In 2000, now splendidly restored, it was put on display in the Victoria and Albert Museum in London.

In place of a screen, there is a central space, with new altar furniture designed by cathedral architect Michael

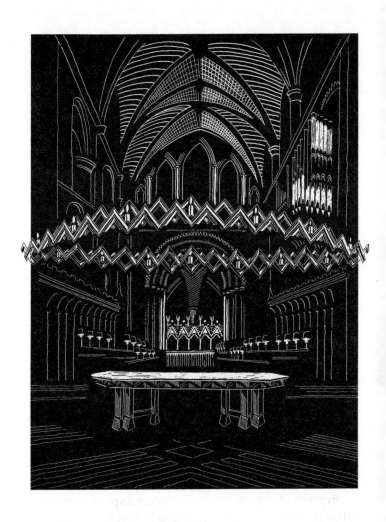

Reardon, and, above the altar, the Corona, designed and made by Simon Beer in 1992, in memory of the late John Eastaugh, Bishop of Hereford from 1974 to 1990.

The Corona picks up several themes. First, the crown of thorns worn by Jesus on the cross. At the altar below the Corona, week by week, we recall the crucified Jesus in Holy Communion and seek strength for the journey. The Corona reflects glory too, and the gold and silver on it gives an image of Christ the King, who promises risen life to his followers. Around the Corona are fourteen candles, symbolizing the fourteen deaneries of the Diocese of Hereford. Thus the life of the Diocese is reflected here at the very heart of the Cathedral where the Holy Communion is celebrated so regularly.

Here are some words by a Muslim writer using the image of the crown of thorns. Anguished by the apparent indifference of God towards the weakness and suffering of the Islamic nations, he uses the same symbol to protest at the tearing apart of his land. He thereby reminds us that this image of self-giving is not peculiar to Christianity.

> *I was not the first to carry a crown of thorns*
> *That I should say: Let me weep.*
> *Could it be that my cross is a steed*
> *and the thorns engraved on my brow*
> *In blood and sweat are a laurel crown?*
> Mahmud Darwish

The Chancel

Here, the praise of God has been sung for centuries. Hereford was not a monastic foundation and so there were no monks in the Cathedral, but the daily round of worship before the Reformation was similar to that in monasteries – not least in that it was performed with great commitment and elaboration. Hereford was one of nine pre-Reformation cathedrals which were staffed by secular priests – the so-called 'Old Foundation Cathedrals': York, Lichfield, St Paul's, Chichester, Wells, Exeter, Salisbury, Lincoln and Hereford. The liturgical systems of York, Hereford and Salisbury were widespread before the Reformation. The 'Use of Hereford' may have had its ancestry in liturgical rites in the Diocese of Rouen in France

These nine cathedrals had communities led by a Dean and Chapter from their earliest days, and the stalls still in daily use in Hereford are those where the worship of God has been sung for almost seven hundred years.

The Bishop's throne dates from the fourteenth century and is a fine example of medieval woodwork. Its size and complexity remind us of the importance of the office of bishop, but Hereford also has a custom which helps to put into perspective authority and power in the Church. Several years ago, Hereford revived the ceremony of the Boy Bishop – a medieval custom whereby a senior chorister is chosen by his peers to dress as a bishop, to officiate alongside the Bishop himself for the period from 6 December (St Nicholas Day) until 28 December (Holy Innocents). During his period of office, the Boy Bishop preachs a sermon, gives blessings and is an important reminder of those words of Jesus, 'Truly I tell you: unless you turn round and become like children, you will never enter the kingdom of Heaven' (Matthew 18.3). Perhaps too we are reminded of the words of Mary in the Magnificat: 'He hath put down the mighty from their seat and hath exalted the humble and meek.'

A prayer for children, especially those for whom we have a special concern – our own children, grand-children and godchildren. We pray for the children in the care of this foundation, especially for our choristers.

Lord God, though you are great, you became a little child in your birth at Bethlehem.
Give us all, like children, your gifts of simplicity, trust and wonder
and lead us, through these, to the very gates of Heaven.

The North Transept

This part of the Cathedral contains excellent examples of thirteenth-century architecture – the huge, soaring western window, and the pointed arches, often said to reflect those dating from the same time in Westminster Abbey.

Nearby is the effigy of Bishop Herbert Westfaling (Bishop of Hereford from 1586 to 1601) lying on his side. An academic, he wrote widely on theological matters and is said to have been very fierce and rather humourless. As Westfaling himself said, 'The staffe or rodde of discipline God hath undoubtedly gyven to all trewe bishops.'

He preached at great length, even when speaking before Queen Elizabeth I. But his running of the Diocese, albeit performed with unsmiling gravity, was nevertheless appreciated. 'I wish', said Bishop Godwin in his book on bishops, 'that our age abounded more in characters of his description.'

Here, we pause awhile to reflect on humour and its vital importance in our lives. So often the Church has been seen as dour and lacking in humour. Yet we find so many instances of humour in the Gospels and we have only to look at some of the carvings in this Cathedral to see that the medieval masons in addition

to being extremely skilful were also men of great wit.
A prayer for the right sort of humour:

*Dear Lord, thank you for calling me to share with others
your precious gift of laughter. May I never forget that it
is your gift and my privilege. As your children are
rebuked in their self-importance and cheered in their
sadness, help me to remember that your foolishness is
wiser than our wisdom.*

'The Clown's Prayer' (source unknown)

Shrine of St Thomas of Hereford in the N. Transept

The Shrine of
St Thomas of Hereford

Thomas Cantilupe was Bishop of Hereford from 1275 to 1282. A man of great piety and devotion, he had a reputation for efficient administration in the Diocese as well as for being unafraid to oppose those who challenged the church's property rights in the Diocese.

A series of disputes over jurisdiction rights with the Archbishop of Canterbury caused his excommunication in 1282 and prompted a personal appeal to Pope Martin IV.

While visiting the papal court in Orvieto, Cantilupe was taken ill and died at Montefiascone in the province of Viterbo on 25 August 1282. His flesh was buried at San Severo in Orvieto and his bones immediately brought back to Hereford where they were buried ina tomb in the Lady Chapel. Shortly before Cantilupe's remains were transferred to the present tomb on Maundy Thursday 1287, a number of miraculous cures were attributed to him. At first largely a local phenomenon, soon many pilgrims began to come to Hereford from more distant regions. Indeed, such were the numbers who came on pilgrimage and for healing that comparison was made between

Hereford's Thomas and the great Thomas Becket at Canterbury.

In 1320 Cantilupe was canonized; his feast day was declared to be 2 October, and special sequences were included in the Hereford liturgy. A sumptuous shrine was built in the Lady Chapel, and in October 1349, after the worst of the Black Death in Hereford was over, his bones were transferred to this shrine in the presence of Edward III. The miracles of healing continued but the cult decreased in popularity and the shrine with its relics was broken up at the Reformation. However, the 1287 shrine – a tomb of Purbeck marble with fourteen knightly members of the Cantilupe family carved on it – is still in the Transept. It is one of very few to survive and is a powerful reminder that we still need holy places to focus our prayers. At the shrine today, candles are lit by our many visitors and pilgrims and prayers are offered – prayers of thanksgiving and prayers for those in need.

At length, the saint from being an innocent lamb was made a good shepherd in the church of Hereford, and ever studying to advance from virtue to virtue from the time when he was placed in so high a position in the temple of God, so shone as to be called the very jewel of Bishops. He went before his sheep to the pastures, defended them from fierce wolves, and led them back to Christ's sheepfolds, fed them by word and example. He stoutly defended the rights of his church, having put on justice as a breastplate. Thus

17

this blessed man, in committing his soul to God, from being a stranger and pilgrim became an illustrious citizen of heaven.

From the Bull of Pope John XXII for the canonization of St Thomas Cantilupe

The Stanbury Chapel

John Stanbury, a Cornishman and Carmelite friar, was confessor to King Henry VI, who founded King's College, Cambridge, and Eton College.

Stanbury was made Bishop of Hereford in 1453 and became one of the most powerful and energetic holders of the see. Under Stanbury, the College of Vicars Choral was rebuilt on a new site to the south-east of the Cathedral. On the Bishop's death at Ludlow, on 11 May 1474, he was buried in his Cathedral. To our right, on the north side of the high altar, is his alabaster tomb, while to our left is the magnificent Chapel, built for masses to be said for the repose of his soul. The Chapel is a superb example of perpendicular architecture, with its fan vaulting and emblematic shields. The chantry was refurnished in the 1920s, and contains brilliantly coloured glass, depicting scenes from Stanbury's life, including those of his enthronement and the foundation of Eton College.

As we remember this great man, and the many prayers said here for his soul, we remember all who have been important in our lives, and whose memory we revere. We remember all who have influenced us on our journey, through their generosity and kindness.

Lord of all, we praise you
for all who have entered into their rest
and reached the promised land where you are seen face to
    face.
Give us grace to follow in their footsteps
as they followed in the way of your Son.
Thank you for the memory of those you have called to
    yourself:
by each memory, turn our hearts from things seen to things
    unseen,
and lead us till we come to the eternal rest you have
    prepared for your people,
through Jesus Christ our Lord.

Common Worship: Pastoral Services
(London: Church House Publishing, 2000)

St Ethelbert, King and Martyr

In the early part of the last decade of the eighth century, Ethelbert, the young King of the East Angles, came to Offa, King of Mercia, to seek the hand of Offa's daughter in marriage. Offa, for political reasons, had Ethelbert murdered. His body was thrown away but was later miraculously discovered and given burial at the site of the Saxon Cathedral at Hereford.

A cult developed at Ethelbert's shrine, and many who sought healing flocked to it. However, when the shrine of St Thomas of Hereford developed in the fourteenth century, Ethelbert's cult declined and there is now little evidence of this former devotion. There are, however, reminders of his existence – a brass, once inlaid on Cantilupe's tomb, a stained-glass window of the fourteenth century and a rather mutilated stone figure, also of the fourteenth century, now near the high altar. Before us is an icon or painting of Ethelbert, and here we remember that martyrs are not only linked to the Church in history: in some parts of the world the costliness of following Christ has never been greater.

Lord Jesus, you experienced in person torture and death as a prisoner of conscience. You were beaten and flogged and sentenced to an agonizing death though you had done no wrong. Be now with prisoners of conscience throughout the world. Be with them in their fear and loneliness, in the agony of physical and mental torture, and in the face of execution and death. Stretch out your hands in power to break their chains. Be merciful to the oppressor and the torturer and place a new heart within them. Forgive all injustice in our lives and transform us to be instruments of your peace, for by your wounds we are healed.

Amnesty International

The Crypt

Much of our visit encourages us to raise our eyes – to look up – to sense the glory.

But the Christian life also has its darkness – its sharing with Christ in his sufferings, its descent to the depths. As we descend the steps to the Crypt, we bring with us times when we have known darkness and the depths. We remember too that the Crypt, even in its darkness, is at the very foundation of the Cathedral and that everything else somehow stems from this foundation. Our own faith needs its foundations and these often emerge from times of darkness and uncertainty.

The Crypt, like the Lady Chapel above it, dates from the early part of the thirteenth century. During its history it has had a variety of uses. In its early days it very likely possessed an altar dedicated to the Holy Trinity, but by the seventeenth century we find the following strange account of its use:

Under the Cathedral-church at Hereford is the greatest charnel-house for bones, that I ever saw in England. In AD 1650, there lived amongst those bones a poor old woman that, to help out her fire, did use to mix the dead-men's bones: this was thrift and poverty: but cunning

The Crypt

alewives putt the Ashes of these bones in their Ale to
make it intoxicating.
Aubrey's *Brief Lives*, ed. Oliver Lawson Dick
(London 1949), p. 24.

During the 1980s the Crypt became a Treasury, for the
display of plate from the churches of the Diocese,
and now it is a chapel set apart for quiet and private
prayer.

It is not difficult to sense the special atmosphere of
this chapel with its dim light and its echoing acoustic.
It now houses a large medieval statue of St John the
Baptist, reminding us of the ancient link between the
parish of St John Baptist and the Cathedral. The parish,
albeit small, still exists, and the Dean is the parish
priest. The statue shows John in his coat of camel
hair, a book in his left hand with a lamb – his symbol –
on it.

And so in the midst of the grandeur of this Cathedral is something really quite small: a small crypt
– a small parish – the smallness of our own prayers
offered in faith. John was a prophet, speaking out
against wrong and evil, and we remind ourselves that
it is often in small things that we are called upon to
make a stand. Often we have no influence over great
decisions on the international stage, but we can nevertheless make our own stand for truth and justice and
for the upholding of human dignity in the workplace,
at home or at school.

Almighty God,
by whose providence your servant John the Baptist was
    wonderfully born,
and sent to prepare the way of your Son our Saviour
by the preaching of repentance:
lead us to repent according to his preaching
and, after his example,
constantly to speak the truth, boldly to rebuke vice,
and patiently to suffer for the truth's sake;
through Jesus Christ your Son our Lord,
who is alive and reigns with you,
in the unity of the Holy Spirit,
one God, now and for ever.

Common Worship
(London: Church House Publishing, 2000)

The Lady Chapel

We now move up the flight of steps and into the light again. The Lady Chapel greets us – a beautiful building dating from about 1220. This too has been used for a variety of purposes in its history. First and foremost it is the site of devotion to Mary, mother of Jesus Christ and the most honoured of all the saints. Behind the altar in the Chapel is a reredos dating from the 1950s, depicting scenes from Mary's life, and on the south side is an icon, where candles are often lit and prayers said. The icon, traditionally created in an atmosphere of prayer, encourages us to stand before it and simply to gaze at the wonder of God being born into our world – at the tenderness and love of mother and son, at the timelessness of faith.

O Christ our God incarnate, whose Virgin Mother was blessed in bearing thee, but still more blessed in keeping thy word: Grant us, who honour the exaltation of her lowliness, to follow the example of her devotion to thy will; who livest and reignest with the Father and the Holy Ghost, ever one God, world without end.
William Bright (1824–1901)

On 25 October 1349, the relics of St Thomas of Hereford were transferred to a new shrine in the presence of King Edward III. The shrine stood in the centre of the Lady Chapel and was destroyed at the Reformation. In 1590 the Lady Chapel was fitted with bookcases and used as the cathedral library; it remained in this use until 1841.

The Chapel has in it some interesting tombs, among them that of John Swinfield, the fourteenth-century Precentor. The tomb has a row of pigs running around the arch above his effigy – a so-called 'rebus' or pun on his name.

If we look around the Cathedral we'll see many examples
of animals carved in stone and wood, often with amusing features. There are some wonderful carvings in St John's walk – a mermaid, a green man. The medieval carver often blended sacred and secular – human, plant and animal life were all parts of God's creation and all had a place in the Cathedral, that great celebration of wholeness and integrity.

Prayer of the Ox

Dear God, give me time,
Men are always so driven!
Make them understand that I can never hurry.
Give me time to eat.
Give me time to plod.
Give me time to sleep.
Give me time to think.
Carmen Bernos de Gasztold (1919–96)

Look out for the Chapel of Bishop Audley, with its beautiful painted screen. Edmund Audley was Bishop of Hereford from 1492 to 1502 and he erected this Chapel as a chantry, where prayers might be said for him after his death. However, he didn't die at Hereford, but was translated to Salisbury as Bishop in 1502, where he died in 1524. At Salisbury he had another chantry chapel built, where he is actually buried.

Looking at Bishop Audley's Chapel makes us ask the question, 'What do we leave when we die?' For Edmund Audley, leaving money for a chantry chapel was a vital part of what he left behind. Indeed, the leaving of money for church building was very common and many of our churches simply wouldn't be there without this generosity.

Some who are buried in the Cathedral may have left little in comparison with the beautiful and elaborate Chapel of Bishop Audley, but often, in their epitaphs,

we can glimpse a little of the humanity and humour in
their lives, which in turn they bequeath to us.

> *RICHARD TOMSON*
> *left in trust*
> *to the Dean and Chapter*
> *of this Cathedral*
> *certain lands for the purpose of*
> *distributing Bread and Money*
> *to 12 poor persons*
> *who shall attend the Choir Service*
> *on the Vigils of Sabbaths*
> *and certain Holy days*
> *to the Deacon having charge*
> *of such distributions*
> *for copying music for the Choir*
> *for clothing certain poor persons*
> *for obtaining discharge*
> *for some poor debtor from prison*
> *and for binding in apprenticeship*
> *some poor boy*
> *brought up a chorister*
> *in this Cathedral.*

A benefaction board in St John's Porch

The South-East Transept

In this part of the Cathedral is one of the most touching memorials in the building.

Herbert Croft became Dean of Hereford in 1644 and, during his ministry, famously preached a dramatic sermon from the pulpit (now seen before us), criticizing the soldiers for their wanton destruction and sacrilege in the Cathedral. During the Commonwealth of the 1650s he was removed from his deanery and driven out, with the other cathedral clergy.

At the Restoration, Croft was made Bishop of Hereford, and a correspondent in *King's Intelligencer* for January 1662 reported: 'the bishop hath won the hearts of all sorts of people'. He encouraged a large restoration of the damaged Cathedral. On his death, at the age of 88, he was buried in the Chancel of the Cathedral, his body soon joined by that of George Benson, who had served with him as dean, who died within fifteen months of the bishop. The slab covering their tombs was removed to the present position and retains the clasped hands – clearly representing a great friendship between these two clerics. The inscription – *In vita coniuncti, in morte non divisi* (united in life, not divided in death) – is a powerful testimony of the enduring nature of real friendship and encourages us at this point to reflect on our own friendships – their richness and variety, friends far from us, friends departed this life, to whom we still feel close. Jesus said to his disciples 'I have called you friends'. So often we fail to see God as friend: we see him as creator, as judge – as above us and not alongside us. This relationship of Jesus to us – as friend and brother – is a vital one.

The friendship between bishop and dean reminds us that such good relations have not always been the norm in cathedral life – from *Barchester Towers* to more recent news stories; cathedrals and great churches, which should be places of warm and outgoing community, had the reputation of not always living up to their vocation.

Be pleased, O Lord, to remember my friends, all that have prayed for me, and all that have done me good.

Do good to them and return all their kindness a double time, rewarding them with blessings and sanctifying them with Thy graces.

Let all my family and kindred, my neighbours and acquaintances receive the benefit of my prayers, and the blessings of God; the comforts and supports of Thy providence, and the sanctification of Thy Spirit.

Jeremy Taylor (1613–1667)

The South Choir Aisle

The overwhelming impression in this part of the Cathedral is of a row of almost identical tombs of former bishops. Their names are known:

William de Vere, 1186–98
Robert Foliot, 1174–86
Robert de Béthune, 1131–48
Robert de Melun, 1163–67

These effigies all date from the fourteenth century, and the occupants of the tombs look very similar indeed – almost as if the tombs were purchased from a catalogue! No doubt there was an accepted effigy for a bishop – the vestments, the mitre, the crozier – and individuality mattered not a great deal.

These tombs in their clear similarity face us with one of the great paradoxes in Christianity. We are called upon to follow Christ – to model ourselves on him, his life and teaching – to be 'Christlike'. We subscribe to doctrines and beliefs in the Church. The priest wears vestments during services to lessen his or her individuality and to emphasize the 'Christlikeness' of the role and ministry. And yet we also glory in the individuality of each person as uniquely made in the image of

God – we encourage discussion and debate and, at its best, the Church is willing to encompass those whose views are not 'the norm'. Indeed, this generosity of approach is what so often marks out a church as opposed to a sect – in the latter, members are very much bound to the letter of belief and practice.

I like these words of the Church of Scotland theologian, Elizabeth Templeton, speaking of the breadth of belief in the Church of England:

> I have been constantly struck by the generosity of your insistence that across parties, camps and dogmas, you have need of each other. Both internally and in relation to other evolving Christian life forms, you have been conspicuously unclassifiable, a kind of ecclesiastical duck-billed platypus, robustly mammal and vigorously egg-laying. That, I am sure, is to be celebrated and not deplored.

The South Transept

Here we see the joining of very different styles and interpretations found in the Christian faith.

The Transept itself is a pure example of early Norman work, with its rounded arches and massive simplicity. In three of the arches are set three tapestries by John Piper, commissioned in 1976 for the 1300th anniversary of the traditional date of the foundation of the Diocese in 676. The tapestries are made by weavers in Namibia, south-west Africa. Old and new are brought together and we are given a contemporary interpretation of three biblical scenes, each involving a tree. While the images are modern, they are strangely timeless as they deal with questions basic to all human beings.

First, on the left, John Piper pictures the Garden of Eden, with its tree of the knowledge of good and evil. We see Adam and Eve, the curled serpent, the forbidden fruit on the tree, the temptation and their expulsion from Paradise. We are brought face to face with the ancient question – why? Why is there sin and wrongdoing in the world? Why do we try to do right but so often do quite the opposite? Is there such a thing as evil? These questions have exercised people through the centuries and we come to the vastness of

South Transept

a building like this with vast questions – seeking perspective, seeking enlightenment.

The next tapestry panel by Piper shows the cross of Jesus Christ as a tree, with the dead Christ being removed from the tree for burial. Christians believe that it was because the human race simply failed to find a way of reconciliation with God that God himself came to earth, to show the way of love and self-giving which is at the heart of the universe. Christians believe that this love and self-giving are seen supremely in the death and resurrection of Jesus Christ. This modern interpretation reminds us that the message of the cross is for all generations, all cultures and all ages.

The third tapestry panel takes us to the Book of Revelation and to John's vision of the Temple in Heaven and its river, flowing with water, on whose banks grows the tree of life.

On either side of the river stood a tree of life, which yields twelve crops of fruit, one for each month of the year. The leaves of the tree are for the healing of the nations.
Revelation 22.1–2

And it is healing that we pray this Cathedral may give to the many who come here as visitors and pilgrims. Healing will come in many different ways: through human contact; through being inspired to pray; through art and music; through silence; through intercession at the shrine of St Thomas.

Above all, these tapestries speak of healing – of the

coming together of different cultures and traditions, of the bridging of ancient and modern. Perhaps this is the ideal place to pray that the healing brought about through Jesus Christ may find a place in our lives too.

A prayer from the sixth century, praising the tree on which hung the crucified Christ:

> *Faithful Cross! above all other,*
> *One and only noble tree!*
> *None in foliage, none in blossom,*
> *None in fruit thy peer may be.*
> *Sweetest wood and sweetest iron,*
> *Sweetest weight is hung on thee.*
> Venantius Fortunatus, 530–609
> (translated from the Latin)

Beneath the tapestries is a crucifix from Tanzania. The Diocese has been linked with four dioceses in Tanzania since the 1980s and there have been many exchange visits and a growing in understanding between our two countries.

We give thanks for all that the African people can teach us about joy and colour in worship, about trust in God, about finding God in poverty and simplicity. Our prayer here is especially for all in Africa caught up in civil war, famine and poverty.

A prayer from Tanzania:

Mungu wetu na baba yetu wa mbinguni na baba wa bwana wetu Yesu Kristo.

Tunakushukuru kwa baraka na neema zako nyingi katika
maisha yetu ya kila siku.

Our heavenly father, we thank you for your grace and
blessing in our daily life.
Thank you for your love and your wonderful grace to us.
David Mnankali, Diocese of Kilimanjaro

A triptych, or three-panelled altarpiece, is placed on
the west wall of the South Transept. Dating from the
sixteenth century, it is a south German piece, depicting the coming of the wise men, or magi, offering their
gifts to the infant Christ. It is a scene of breaking down
of barriers. By this action the wise men seem to be
proclaiming Christianity as something inclusive and
open, free from prejudice and fear.

Our prayer here is that all who come to the
Cathedral may find that same acceptance and openness both in worship and in the welcome they receive.

O God,
who by the leading of a star
manifested your only Son to the peoples of the earth:
mercifully grant that we,
who know you now by faith,
may at last behold your glory face to face;
through Jesus Christ your Son our Lord.
Common Worship
(London: Church House Publishing, 2000)

Mappa Mundi and the Chained Library

Our visit to the Cathedral has brought us into touch with many world cultures: we have experienced the Cathedral's Norman (French) architecture; we have prayed at the shrine of the Cathedral's English patron saint; we have seen links with Namibia, with Tanzania and Germany.

We place together all these different cultures as we focus on the world in its totality and as we come now to the Cathedral's greatest treasure. Mappa Mundi – a map of the world – dates from the end of the thirteenth century. Created by Richard of Haldingham or Lafford (or Holdingham or Sleaford, in Lincolnshire), the map has probably been in the Cathedral's possession for hundreds of years. In the past ten years, its significance has been even more greatly realized, with its being housed in a dedicated building and with an exhibition to interpret and set it in its historical context.

On our pilgrimage, Mappa Mundi calls us to reflect on the world in which we live. In so many ways, the world of Richard of Haldingham and our own world are utterly different. We now know so much more about our planet and its workings – space travel has enabled us to see the earth in relation to other parts of the universe and modern developments in science have unlocked so many things simply mysterious and unfathomable to the thirteenth-century mind. And yet, in other ways, the world is the same and development has been limited.

Jerusalem·

The world of Mappa Mundi looks small and fragile, as indeed it still is today, and lack of care for our planet has emphasized its fragility and vulnerability. Mappa Mundi shows Jerusalem as the centre of the world – the creator of the map is putting something spiritual at the centre of the world. Today we so often put ourselves and our selfish needs at the centre of worlds of our own making.

Mappa Mundi is peppered with images of beasts, described in travellers' tales. We may see them today

Leopard·

as 'mythical', even naive, but they were as real to the map's author as those we know to be 'real': all are accompanied by bits of text which are authoritative according to the contemporary state of knowledge of the world.

In fact the human psyche is still plagued by dark mysteries and unknown forces, and while science has brought many wonderful developments it has not

Salamandra·

provided all the answers in the hundreds of years since the map was created.

Over Mappa Mundi presides the figure of Christ. The author of this map is making a strong theological statement here about the place of God in the cosmos. The Christian looks forward to the day when Christ's rule will be over the whole world. This is not to make assumptions about the superiority of Christianity but is, I think, a prayer that Christ's rule of peace, justice and self-giving will one day find a place in the hearts of all, and that men and women will be united in their search for truth.

And so, as we stand before Mappa Mundi, a prayer for the feast of Christ the King:

Eternal Father,
Whose Son Jesus Christ ascended to the throne of heaven
*   that he might rule over the world as Lord and King:*
keep the Church in the unity of the Spirit
and in the bond of peace,
and bring the whole created order to worship at his feet;
who is alive and reigns with you,
in the unity of the Holy Spirit,
one God, now and for ever.

Common Worship
(London: Church House Publishing, 2000)

A page from the Hereford Gospels

No visit to the Cathedral would be complete without a visit to the Chained Library. Containing some 1,500 volumes, the library is a unique survival and is visited by scholars from all over the world. The Cathedral has been a centre of learning since its earliest times and some of the books in the library today have been in the Cathedral's possession since the twelfth century. Chief among these are the Hereford Gospels, thought to have been given to the Cathedral by Athelstan, Bishop of Hereford from 1012 to 1056. This priceless treasure is used for the swearing of oaths at the enthronement of bishops and the installation of deans; it reminds us of the long and unbroken Christian tradition and witness in this place.

In addition, there is a working library of over 10,000 volumes, including the modern lending and reference library. These ancient and modern resources remind us that Christianity, along with Islam and Judaism, is a major 'religion of the book'. In these faith communities, the scriptures are given special honour as recording great events of faith. Books have been used through the centuries both to interpret these scriptures and to reflect on God and on the experience of those who hold to these faiths.

Yet, as we value the books and their wisdom, we are reminded that the Christian has to balance both the 'letter' and the 'spirit'. When Christianity has over-emphasized 'the book' it has often led to a rigid and unyielding interpretation. And Christians who have undervalued the power of 'the book' have often failed to give honour to the tradition and stability of the faith.

> *There is much else that Jesus did. If it were all to be recorded in detail, I suppose the world could not hold the books that would be written.*
> John 21.25

The Chapter House Garden

The Chapter House – the place where the community gathered to meet – was in ruins by the eighteenth century, and on its site is this lovely garden where, in the summer, visitors gather to enjoy the sunshine and to eat and drink.

As we pause in the beauty of this spot, we recall significant times when gardens are mentioned in the Bible:

The Garden of Eden reminds us of our quest for goodness in a world where so much speaks of a fall from paradise and a failure to find truth and justice.

The Garden of Gethsemane, scene in Jerusalem of Jesus' agony and betrayal. This reminds us of a world where, so often, people fail to 'watch and wait' with those enduring pain and agony in their own lives – a world where people are betrayed, often by those closest to them.

The Garden of the Resurrection, scene on the first Easter morning of Jesus Christ appearing to his disciples, to show them that death is not the end.

This garden reminds us that, through Christ, we can find eternal life.

All these gardens – of failure, of betrayal, of goodness, of new life – we gather together in our thoughts as we keep silence and listen to the sounds around us.

God of growth, truth and beauty,
help us to find you wherever you are –
when we fail – when we are betrayed –
when we know death – when we know life.
Weave together all our experiences and
help us in them all to see your compassion and love.
Through Jesus Christ our Lord.

The College of Vicars Choral

Being a Cathedral of the Old Foundation, Hereford never had monks to lead worship. Instead, 'secular' priests were involved, organized as a college, who lived and worked together, and while not bound by monastic vows nevertheless led a disciplined life similar in some respects to that of their monastic brothers.

The first building of the College of Vicars Choral was near to the present Castle Street, some two hundred yards from the Cathedral. Complaints from the Vicars about their living conditions led to the building of a new college in 1472–75 by Bishop Stanbury. The College is built around a Cloister and originally had accommodation for 24 priests. There was a chapel for their use, and a kitchen and dining hall. A narrow corridor, St John's Walk, joins the College directly to the Cathedral. This had the advantage not only of enabling the Vicars to reach the church in the dry but also obviated any unnecessary communication with townspeople who might gather at the entrance to the Cathedral.

After the Reformation, while monastic foundations were invariably destroyed, the College continued its life, relatively unchanged. The number of Vicars decreased and there are now no such office-holders living in the Cloister. However, the Cloister is still the centre of a community, and in it are found the cathedral offices as well as homes for the Dean, the vergers and the cathedral musicians. Certainly the life of the Cloister is more integrated with the life of the Cathedral today. Until the nineteenth century the college functioned almost entirely independently, and there were frequent disputes between the Vicars and the Dean and Chapter. The Vicars had their own constitution and their own lands, and there was little concept of 'overlapping communities'.

Community is certainly at the Cathedral's heart. From earliest times, the Cathedral has been governed by a Chapter – a community in miniature. Now consisting of lay and ordained members, the Chapter is supported by a much larger community – a permanent staff and an army of volunteers, who help in many different ways: guiding and welcoming, flower-arranging, serving in the cathedral shop and café, cleaning, bell-ringing. Each church seeks to be a living example of 'the Body of Christ', but perhaps the Cathedral, in its role as the mother church of the Diocese, has a special task to enhance this vital concept of community.

On many occasions throughout the year, the community is enlarged, as we welcome those who use the Cathedral for concerts and other events. When the cathedral choir is on holiday, the services are sung by visiting choirs, and these have a vital part to play in continuing the community's ministry of worship.

Every three years the Cathedral hosts the annual Three Choirs Festival, begun in the eighteenth century which, while still providing opportunities for the three choirs of Gloucester, Hereford and Worcester to sing together, is now an international festival, with a week's concerts and activities, during which the cathedral community is hugely expanded.

The Cathedral welcomes over 200,000 visitors each year, and our hope is that all who come will not only see themselves as visiting an ancient building, but will sense themselves as part of a living, developing community in which all are welcome.

So, as we pause in the peace of the Cloister in the College of Vicars Choral, we remember all the communities of which we are part: our families, our networks of friendship, our work, our school, our town and neighbourhood communities, our hobbies and interests; and while we thank God for the support that these communities give, we remember those who have no recognizable community: those who are exiled from all that is familiar to them; all who know isolation and who lack the warmth of human community. We pray that this Cathedral may be able to continue in this vital work of supporting community in all aspects.

We are the body of Christ.
In one Spirit we were all baptized into one body.
Endeavour to keep the unity of the Spirit
in the bond of peace.

The peace of the Lord be always with you.